Iris Folding

for Life's Special Moments™

Follow your dreams till they take wing and fly

Annie's™

Iris Folding for Life's Special Moments

EDITOR Tanya Fox
CREATIVE DIRECTOR Brad Snow
PUBLISHING SERVICES DIRECTOR Brenda Gallmeyer
MANAGING EDITOR Brooke Smith
GRAPHIC DESIGNER Nick Pierce
COPY SUPERVISOR Corene Painter
TECHNICAL EDITORS Corene Painter, Läna Schurb
COPY EDITORS Emily Carter, Rebecca Detwiler
PRODUCTION ARTIST SUPERVISOR Erin Brandt
PRODUCTION ARTIST Nicole Gage
PRODUCTION ASSISTANTS Marj Morgan, Judy Neuenschwander
PHOTOGRAPHY SUPERVISOR Tammy Christian
PHOTO STYLISTS Tammy Liechty, Tammy Steiner
PHOTOGRAPHY Matthew Owen

Iris Folding for Life's Special Moments is published by Annie's, 306 East Parr Road, Berne, IN 46711. Printed in USA. Copyright © 2013 Annie's. All rights reserved. This publication may not be reproduced in part or in whole without written permission from the publisher.

RETAIL STORES: If you would like to carry this pattern book or any other Annie's publication, visit AnniesWSL.com.

Every effort has been made to ensure that the instructions in this publication are complete and accurate. We cannot, however, take responsibility for human error, typographical mistakes or variations in individual work. Please visit AnniesCustomerCare.com to check for pattern updates.

ISBN: 978-1-59635-583-5

Printed in the USA

1 2 3 4 5 6 7 8 9

Contents

Welcome to *Iris Folding for Life's Special Moments*, my second book on iris folding—and my fourth book on paper-crafting techniques. The first iris-folding book, comprised solely of Christmas-themed cards, was a joy to bring together, just like the season it reflected. This book was equally exciting to work on, affording me the opportunity to expand my horizons by designing with many themes in mind. These themes cover a variety of occasions and moments in one's life when a beautiful greeting card would be appreciated and appropriate.

On this creative journey, you will discover both traditional and nontraditional iris-folding designs, and you will have the opportunity to use a variety of materials, such as paper, fabric, ribbon and Mylar, as you create them. You will learn how to mix and match patterns with apertures to get more mileage from your patterns and explore some "outside the box" design ideas like turning a teacup-shaped aperture (opening) into a flower and even a party dress!

Many popular card-making products have been combined with the iris-folding technique on these pages. However, if you do not have the exact products listed, don't worry. Follow the instructions for the basic design and use what you have. It's always nice to personalize cards by using your favorite colors, images and words, so please don't be afraid to experiment once you have mastered the technique.

They say it takes a village to raise a child. This is also true when it comes to creating a book! Many talented individuals have played important roles in creating this book. From photography to editing and everything in between, your efforts are truly appreciated. My sincere thanks to the team at Annie's!

My heartfelt thanks also to the teams at Quietfire Design, Scor-Pal Products and Spellbinders™ Paper Arts, not only for creating wonderful products that are a joy to use, but also for providing product support for this book!

It is my hope that as you celebrate the special moments of your life and the people who have touched your life, you will not only make use of the card projects found in these pages, but you will also be inspired!

Creatively yours,

Introduction to Iris Folding

The iris-folding technique is a paper craft that originated in Holland and takes its name from the signature spiral effect that is created when the paper strips have been adhered. The finished design resembles the iris of an eye or camera.

When this craft first originated, the printed liners inside envelopes, somewhat like our security envelopes today, were cut and folded to create the strips used to create the intricate designs.

Over the years, this beautiful technique has evolved far beyond the insides of envelopes—and beyond paper, for that matter. The projects in this book explore both traditional and nontraditional methods and materials.

Iris folding is impressive, yet the designs are easier to create than a first glance would lead you to believe. The technique involves only a few simple steps: creating a frame with an aperture (opening), folding strips of lightweight paper in half (or cutting strips of heavier paper), and following a pattern to adhere the strips in place.

Tools & Materials

As with any craft, there are some specific tools that are required for iris folding and others that make the process easier. Assembling a basic paper-crafting tool kit is recommended. Depending on the types of projects that will be created, the kit will vary from person to person. Basic tools that are helpful for card makers to include are scissors, a bone folder, piercing tool and mat, pencil, various adhesives and a paper trimmer.

Papers

Traditionally, lightweight papers that can be folded easily have been used for iris folding. Papers such as gift wrap, tissue paper, photocopy paper, stationery, origami and chiyogami papers work wonderfully. As we mentioned earlier, don't forget that the insides of security envelopes can be used for iris folding; book prints and recycled papers are equally effective.

A plethora of other beautiful heavier-weight papers, such as patterned cardstocks and handmade papers, can also be used. Though they may be too heavy to use in the traditional folded form, they work very well when they are simply cut into strips—and this has the added advantage of speeding up the process. Although this is a step away from the traditional method, the same signature spiral effect can be achieved.

Both printed and solid-color papers can be used in iris folding. Solid-colored papers can be transformed with the use of stamps. Adding subtle texture to your paper through the use of embossing folders is another great option that will lead to stunning results.

Quilling strips are a great example of a nontraditional material that can be used to create beautiful results. Available in beautiful pearlescent colors and varying widths, quilling strips are usually light enough to fold—or you can simply use a suitably narrow width and omit folding altogether.

Beyond Paper

Paper is not the only material that can be used to create iris-folded designs. The many beautiful ribbons that are available can be used to striking effect. Using ribbon can also be a timesaver, as part of the preparation already has been completed—there are no strips to cut! Many paper lines have coordinating ribbons, which makes choosing color combinations a breeze.

Visit any fabric store to discover bolt after bolt of beautiful fabric just waiting to be showcased in an iris-folded design. In this book, No-Sew Beautiful (page 18) is a great project that makes use of wonderful fabrics.

Quilting stores are great, even for nonquilters; the color and print combinations they display to inspire quilters can be just as inspirational to paper crafters. It's twice as nice for iris folding; the inspiration is provided, and you won't need much fabric to complete an iris-folded design.

Fabric can easily be combined with paper strips to create stunning iris-fold designs. Or, simply use coordinating fabrics to create the entire design as demonstrated on No-Sew Beautiful (page 18)—three prints are from a collection that already has been designed to work together, and the fourth was chosen to coordinate with one of the colors in the striped print. The possibilities are truly endless!

To give fabric a bit more body, the use of spray starch is recommended. The starch should be applied before cutting the strips to create a smooth, crisp surface, and

it can be reapplied to the 1-inch-wide strips before they are folded and ironed. Starch not only lends body but also produces a sharp crease along the folded edge.

In this book, frames with apertures (openings) are often used to create the iris-folded design; the frames are then adhered to the card using foam mounting tape. This is the perfect adhesive product for giving added dimension and depth, but it is also excellent for applying those items that are a bit bulkier than paper, such as ribbon, fabric and Mylar. Mylar sheets, such as the Shimmer Sheetz™ used in one of the projects, make for beautiful designs and are easily cut with scissors or a paper trimmer.

Iris Embellishments

Many of these projects include some type of embellishment as a finishing accent. When choosing an embellishment, coordinate it with the card itself through color, texture, shape or even words that complement the card. Among the many items that make beautiful accents for the iris center are rhinestones, pearls, flowers, buttons, stamped images, ribbons, bows, photographs, sewing notions like snaps, thread-wrapped cardstock shapes, rub-on transfers, stickers, gems, mosaic tiles, beads and pieces from recycled or broken jewelry.

Adhesives

Several types of adhesives are helpful to use when iris folding. These include Scor-Tape double-sided adhesive in ¼- and ⅛-inch widths. This tape has a liner, and it's great for assembling cards; the ¼-inch width is perfect for using around the aperture.

Painter's tape, a low-tack tape, or removable tape is a must-have for securing iris-folding frames to the patterns.

Cellophane tape is usually used to adhere the paper strips. However, when using heavier materials, like fabric or ribbon, using both cellophane tape and double-sided adhesive is often recommended.

Scotch®/3M Foam Mounting Tape is used extensively with these projects, not only for the frames but also to give depth and dimension to other areas of the card.

A liquid glue such as Tombow® Mono Multi liquid glue is another popular "go-to" adhesive as it bonds in two ways: permanent if items are adhered while the adhesive is still wet; repositionable if the adhesive is allowed to dry before items are attached. There are also dual applicators. The pen point is perfect to use with small items while the broad point is suitable to use on larger pieces. This adhesive can be used on a number of embellishments, such as gems, flowers and cabochons, and dries clear.

There are many other types of adhesives that can make different processes easier. Adhesive dots, glue pens and a Xyron sticker maker are all great options to have on hand. As you expand your iris-folding experiences, you'll find that the range of adhesives you like to use will also grow.

Cutting Tools

The basics here are sharp scissors and a paper trimmer. Paper strips are easily cut with a paper trimmer—and the handy measurement guidelines are right there for you. As an alternative, you can use a craft knife, metal-edge ruler and cutting mat.

For fabrics, a rotary trimmer (handheld or the trimmer style) is recommended. Besides cutting fabric, it's the perfect tool for cutting some of the more fibrous handmade papers.

Patterns

A pattern is recommended for creating a traditional iris-folded design. Patterns are available in many shapes and sizes, from basic shapes and beyond. There is even a line of rubber stamps specifically for iris folding. The Merry & Bright card (page 16) uses this style of stamp.

A Pattern Gallery of assorted images is provided on pages 47–48 and includes square patterns in a variety of sizes as well as a heart, triangle and octagon. A butterfly pattern is also included in the form of a numbering diagram for the card Follow Your Dreams (page 44).

Many patterns can be used for apertures of different shapes. In this book, we "mix and match" to get more mileage out of the patterns.

The triangle pattern is a perfect example. It can be used for a leaf, teacup, flower, party dress, Christmas tree or banner.

Simply center your opening over the pattern, and count the number of strips in each section to make them equal if possible. Some projects, however, have different numbers of strips in different sections and still look beautiful. Explore the possibilities!

Some patterns included here have been numbered where needed. However, most of the patterns in this book are not numbered. This allows you the option of customizing the pattern to the materials you are working with, placing a name or color code on the pattern, or leaving it blank. For the most part, once the first round of strips has been placed, a color code has been established. So numbering the pattern is often not necessary, unless further direction is required.

You can also create your own patterns. Working on graph paper is a great way to start.

Choose your perimeter shape—square, circle, oval, Christmas tree, whatever you choose. Most often, the strips of paper are ½ inch wide, but ribbons are often ⅜ inch wide. A pattern created with ¼- to ⅜-inch spaces is quite versatile and will also work for wider strips.

Draw your perimeter shape. Then measure and mark the amount of space you want to have between pattern lines. In the diagrams shown on the next page, a ⁵⁄₁₆-inch space has been used. Make a mark at each side, then connect the mark with lines. Continue in the same manner, measuring and marking for each consecutive round until the pattern is complete. See the diagrams on the next page.

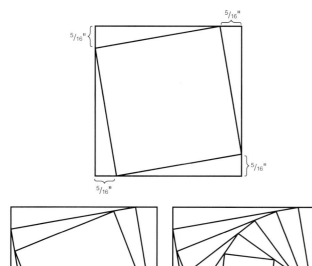

Iris Folding
How to Draw a Pattern

Getting Started

To achieve the best results, paper strips must be cut and folded accurately. The width of the strips can vary, but for most designs, ⅜- to ½-inch-wide strips work well. Trim the strips as necessary for more intricate, detailed designs or for using within smaller frames.

Once the strips are cut, if you are using lightweight paper, the next step is to fold them in half lengthwise. If you are using cardstock or heavier paper, you can simply cut the strips to the desired width and length without folding.

For the projects in this book, you'll use 1-inch-wide strips if they need to be folded and ½-inch-wide strips that need only to be cut.

Creating a Frame With an Aperture

There are several methods for creating a frame with an aperture, or window. The manual method shown here is only one way, and this can be combined with the use of a die.

Punches are another option; however, their reach is limited unless they are the style that can be punched anywhere on the page.

One of the quickest and most accurate methods is to use a die-cutting system and die templates. Several

systems on the market work very well to create apertures. Spellbinders™, Sizzix and Provo Craft have their own die-cutting systems.

Other options for frames with apertures include slide mounts, laser-cut wooden frames, precut window cards and mat board frames.

Follow these steps to create your own iris-folding frame with an aperture.

1. Cut a square of cardstock to the desired size.

2. On the back of the square, draw diagonal lines from corner to corner.

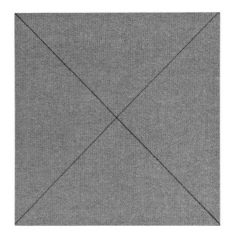

3. Cut a square of cardstock the desired size for the aperture.

4. Place this square onto the back of the larger square, aligning the corners to the diagonal lines. (This is a quick way to center your opening.)

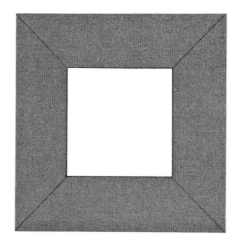

5. Trace around the smaller square with a pencil. Cut out using a craft knife, metal-edge ruler and cutting mat. If cutting with a die, align the corners of the die with the diagonal lines. Apply a small piece of removable tape to hold the die in place while die-cutting.

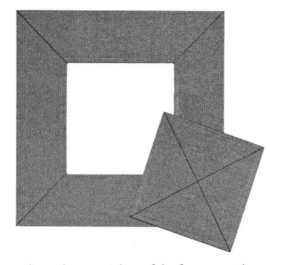

You can leave the outer edges of the frame straight, or use different techniques, such as tearing, distressing with sandpaper or ink, cutting with decorative-edge scissors, or using border dies and punches.

Keep in mind that you can change the size of the iris-folding frame simply by enlarging or reducing the size of the aperture and frame.

Adding the Strips

To begin creating an iris-folding design, you will need a pattern to follow. Photocopy or stamp the pattern onto cardstock, a sticky note, paper, vellum or a transparency sheet. Use removable tape to secure the pattern to a cutting mat or other work surface. Tape the frame with the aperture right side down onto the pattern, centering the pattern in the opening.

Following the project instructions, place the first paper strip right side down, aligning the edge with the line on the pattern. Use cellophane tape to adhere the strip to the frame. Cut off excess from paper strip at the opposite end and secure with tape.

Note: *Keep in mind that you are adding one strip at a time to the back of the aperture, starting at the outer edges and working toward the center to build the pattern. Remember that you are working on the back of the iris fold; once completed and turned right side up, your finished iris fold will be revealed.*

Unnumbered patterns can be worked clockwise or counterclockwise, as long as you remain consistent throughout the project. The projects in this book have been worked counterclockwise. Refer to the project photo as needed.

Beyond the Basics

Once you have mastered basic iris-folding techniques, explore some of the fun alternative approaches. Patterns may be worked in their entirety, filling all the spaces; or only a few rows of strips may be adhered, leaving room in the center for a stamped image, photo, quotation, or other embellishment.

As you become more familiar with iris folding, make use of the other paper-crafting tools and supplies in your "stash." Don't be afraid to experiment! That's usually how the "next best thing" is discovered.

Forever

. . . .

1. Form a 5½-inch-square card from silver cardstock; set aside.

2. For dual frame, cut a 4¾-inch square of purple cardstock. Referring to photo, die-cut two 1⅞ x 2-inch hearts in cardstock.

3. Position Heart Pattern on work surface; place frame facedown on pattern, centering pattern in one of the openings. Secure with removable tape.

4. Apply double-sided adhesive around edges of opening; peel protective liner strip from adhesive.

5. Cut five 1 x 6-inch strips each from silver text-weight paper, Wedding Words paper and tissue paper; fold each strip in half lengthwise.

6. Place Wedding Words strip at bottom right, aligning folded edge with pattern line. Adhere one end with tape; trim excess and secure opposite end.

7. In the same manner, position a silver strip across top; adhere. Adhere a tissue-paper strip at left. Continue working around pattern until all areas are filled except center triangle.

8. Carefully remove pattern from frame. Repeat steps 3–7 to work iris-folded pattern in second die-cut opening. Adhere 2½" x 21/2" Squares of purple sparkle tissue paper over iris-folded designs. Turn frame panel faceup.

9. Adhere iris-folded panel to a 5¼-inch square of Wedding Words paper. Referring to photo, wrap ribbon around assembled panel, positioning knot toward top. Adhere panel to card front.

10. Stamp sentiment onto white cardstock using flannel gray ink. Die-cut a 2⅝ x 2¾-inch Heart around sentiment; ink edges with pretty petunia and flannel gray. Adhere heart to card front as shown using foam mounting tape. ●

Materials
- Heart Pattern (page 48)
- Cardstock: Bazzill Basics (purple textured, white smooth); Stardream (metallic silver)
- Michaels Recollections Wedding Words patterned paper
- Stardream metallic text-weight paper: silver
- Tissue paper: silver/white swirl, purple sparkle
- Quietfire Design Together Forever stamp
- Ink pads: Clearsnap Ancient Page dye (flannel gray); Imagine Crafts/Tsukineko VersaMagic (pretty petunia)
- May Arts ⅜-inch-wide charcoal sheer iridescent pinstripe ribbon
- Spellbinders™ Classic Heart die templates (#S4-136)
- Sizzix Big Shot die-cutting machine
- Bone folder
- Scotch®/3M Foam Mounting Tape
- Removable tape
- Scor-Pal ¼-inch-wide double-sided adhesive
- Tape

Congratulations

1. Form a 5½ x 4¼-inch card from pink polka-dot cardstock. Die-cut a 2½ x 2¼-inch Nested Duck from center of card front.

2. Lay open card facedown on 2½" x 2½" Square Pattern, positioning as shown on Aperture Placement & Numbering Guide; secure with removable tape.

3. Apply double-sided adhesive around edges of opening; peel protective liner strip from adhesive.

4. Cut six ½ x 4-inch strips and two ½ x 4¼-inch strips from ivory paper; emboss with hearts; emboss with hearts embossing folder. Set aside 4¼-inch strips for card front.

Materials

- 2½" x 2½" Square Pattern (page 47)
- Cardstock: Canvas Corp. (pink polka-dot); Stardream (ivory pearlescent)
- Stardream ivory pearlescent text-weight paper
- Paplin ½-inch-wide pearl pink quilling paper strips
- Studio G Congrats stamp
- Embossing ink pad
- Silver embossing powder
- American Crafts Elements pastel pink pearl brad
- ¼-inch-wide cream sheer ribbon
- Spellbinders™ Nested Ducks die templates (#S4-262)
- Crafts-Too Hearts embossing folder (#CTFD3018)
- Sizzix Big Shot die-cutting machine
- Oval cutter
- Paper-piercing tool
- Embossing heat tool
- Bone folder
- Scotch®/3M Foam Mounting Tape
- Removable tape
- Scor-Pal ¼-inch-wide double-sided adhesive
- Tape

5. Referring to Aperture Placement & Numbering Guide throughout, position a pink quilling strip right side down on position 1, aligning edge with line on pattern. Adhere one end with tape; trim excess and adhere opposite end.

6. Position an embossed ivory 4-inch strip right side down at right side, on position 2. Adhere one end with tape; trim excess and adhere opposite end. In the same manner, adhere quilling strip at position 3 and embossed strip at 4.

7. Continue working pattern in numerical order, adhering embossed strips and quilling strips, until all areas are filled except for center square. ***Note:*** *Follow the order on the Numbering Guide carefully. Strips 1, 3, 5, 7, 10, 12, 13, 15, 17 and 19 are quilling strips; strips 2, 4, 6, 8, 9, 11, 14, 16 and 18 are embossed.*

8. Cut a 1½-inch square from pink polka-dot cardstock; adhere to back of center opening using double-sided adhesive.

9. Carefully remove pattern from frame; turn frame faceup.

10. Pierce hole through center of iris; insert pastel pink brad. Adhere reserved 4¼-inch embossed strips to card front as shown.

11. Stamp "congrats" onto ivory pearlescent cardstock; sprinkle embossing powder over sentiment and heat-emboss. Cut a 2 x ⅞-inch oval around sentiment; adhere to card front as shown using foam mounting tape.

12. Cut a 5¼ x 4-inch piece from ivory paper; center and adhere inside card, covering iris-folded design, using double-sided adhesive. Tie ribbon around top of card front as shown. ●

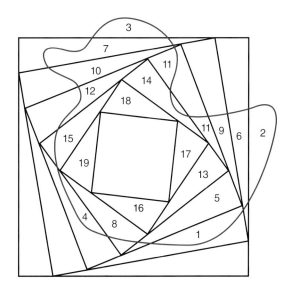

Congratulations
Aperture Placement & Numbering Guide

Thinking of You

Materials

- 2½" x 2½" Square Pattern (page 47)
- The Japanese Paper Place sea blue linen cardstock
- The Paper Loft Easy Breezy Okey Dokey Artichokey patterned paper
- Stardream ivory pearlescent text-weight paper
- Stardream gold heavyweight vellum
- Paplin ½-inch-wide pearl robin's egg blue quilling strip
- Gina K. Designs Framed Greetings stamp set
- Clearsnap ColorBox chestnut roan Fluid Chalk ink pad
- 3 tiny yellow rhinestone flowers
- Spellbinders™ die templates: Classic Squares LG (#S4-126), Lacey Squares (#S4-295)
- Provo Craft Cuttlebug Plum Blossom embossing folder set (#20-00236)
- Sizzix Big Shot die-cutting machine
- Fiskars Apron Lace border punch (#145970-1001)
- Oval cutter
- Bone folder
- Scotch®/3M Foam Mounting Tape
- Removable tape
- Scor-Pal ¼-inch-wide double-sided adhesive
- Tape

1. Form a 4¼ x 5½-inch card from sea blue cardstock; set aside.

2. For frame, cut a 3¾ x 5-inch piece of patterned paper; die-cut a 2½-inch Classic Squares LG from paper as shown.

3. Die-cut a 3¼-inch Lacey Squares from sea blue linen cardstock; die-cut a 2½-inch Classic Square from center of square, creating a lacy border. Adhere border around frame opening.

4. Lay frame facedown on 2½" x 2½" Square Pattern, centering pattern in opening; secure with removable tape.

5. Apply double-sided adhesive around edges of opening; peel protective liner strip from adhesive.

6. Cut quilling strip into five 4-inch pieces; emboss with floral design embossing folder. Cut two ½ x 12-inch strips from patterned paper and three ½ x 11-inch strips each from ivory paper and gold vellum.

7. Place an embossed strip right side down at bottom right, aligning edge with pattern line. Adhere one end with tape; trim excess and secure opposite end.

8. In the same manner, position an ivory strip at top right; adhere. Adhere a patterned paper strip at top left and gold vellum strip at bottom left. Continue working around pattern until all areas are filled except center square.

9. Cut a 1¾-inch square from sea blue linen cardstock; adhere to back of center opening using double-sided adhesive.

10. Carefully remove pattern from frame, and turn frame panel faceup. Adhere rhinestone flower to iris center.

11. Cut a 3½ x ½-inch strip of gold vellum; punch ends using border punch as shown. Adhere to frame panel as shown.

12. Stamp sentiment onto smooth side of sea blue cardstock. Cut a 2 x ⅞-inch oval around sentiment; adhere to vellum strip on frame panel. Adhere rhinestone flowers to oval.

13. Adhere iris-folded panel to card front using foam mounting tape. ●

Elegance

1. Form a 5½-inch-square card from black linen cardstock.

2. Cut a 4¼-inch square of Chiyogami paper; using double-sided adhesive, adhere to a 5⅛-inch-square piece of ice gold cardstock, and adhere to card front. Set aside.

3. For frame, die-cut a 4 x 4-inch Frame from black linen cardstock. Reserve center square die cut.

4. Lay frame facedown on 2½" x 2½" Square Pattern, centering pattern in opening; secure with removable tape.

5. Apply double-sided adhesive around edges of opening; peel protective liner strip from adhesive.

6. Cut three ½ x 8½-inch strips from anthracite paper and ice gold cardstock. Cut three 1 x 8½-inch strips from Chiyogami and gold Midare papers; fold only 1-inch paper strips in half lengthwise.

7. Place a Chiyogami strip right side down at bottom right, aligning folded edge with pattern line. Adhere one end with tape; trim excess and secure opposite end.

8. In the same manner, position an anthracite paper strip at top right, then a gold Midare strip at top left, and an ice gold cardstock strip at bottom left. Continue working around pattern until five strips have been placed in each section.

9. Adhere reserved black cardstock square from step 2 to back of center opening using double-sided adhesive.

10. Carefully remove pattern from frame; turn frame panel faceup.

11. Pierce hole through center of iris; insert brad. Center and adhere iris-folded panel to card using foam mounting tape. ●

Materials

- 2½" x 2½" Square Pattern (page 47)
- Cardstock: The Paper Company™/ TPC Studio™ (black linen); Arjo Wiggins Curious Metallics (ice gold)
- The Japanese Paper Place patterned papers: Chiyogami (#31C), gold Midare
- Stardream anthracite metallic text-weight paper
- Gartner Studios pearl brad
- Sizzix Originals Frame die template (#654988)
- Sizzix Big Shot die-cutting machine
- Paper-piercing tool
- Bone folder
- Scotch®/3M Foam Mounting Tape
- Removable tape
- Scor-Pal ¼-inch-wide double-sided adhesive
- Tape

Birthday Wishes

1. Form an 8½ x 4-inch card from indigo cardstock. Adhere a 6 x 3¼-inch piece of blue/green/white septagon patterned cardstock to card front as shown. Die-cut two ⅞ x 2¾-inch Nested Pennant Ribbons from green/white patterned cardstock; adhere to card front as shown. Set card aside.

2. For frame, cut a 3¾-inch square of indigo cardstock; die-cut a 2-inch square on the diagonal from center; reserve die-cut piece. Punch four photo corners from green/white patterned cardstock; adhere to corners of frame.

3. Position 2" x 2" Square Pattern on work surface. Place frame facedown on pattern with pattern centered in opening; secure with removable tape.

4. Apply double-sided adhesive around edges of opening; peel protective liner strip from adhesive.

5. Cut four ½ x 6-inch strips each from green/white print, blue/green/white septagon print, blue/green/white argyle print and light blue/white microdot patterned cardstock. ***Note:*** *For a pleasing effect, choose two bold patterns and two more subtle patterns; alternate placement between bold and subtle.*

6. Place an argyle strip at bottom right, aligning edge with pattern line. Adhere one end with tape; trim excess and secure opposite end.

7. In the same manner, position a light blue/white microdot strip at top right; adhere. Adhere a septagon print strip at top left, and a green/white print strip at bottom left. Continue working around pattern until all areas are filled except center square.

8. Adhere reserved square die cut from step 2 to back of center opening using double-sided adhesive. Carefully remove pattern from frame; turn frame panel faceup.

9. Punch a ½-inch circle from one of the previously unused papers in the bundle. Apply liquid glue to back of cabochon; adhere cabochon to punched circle; let dry. ***Note:*** *Glue will dry clear.* Once dry, adhere cabochon to iris center. Adhere iris-folded panel to card with foam mounting tape.

10. Stamp sentiment onto microdot cardstock. Cut a rectangle around sentiment and adhere to card as shown. ●

Materials
- 2" x 2" Square Pattern (page 48)
- Neenah Classic Columns indigo cardstock
- Authentique Loyal Collection 6 x 6-inch patterned cardstock bundle
- Gina K. Designs Framed Greetings stamp set
- Ranger Distress faded jeans ink pad
- Ecogreen Crafts Glass Glintz 12mm clear round cabochon
- Spellbinders™ die templates: Nested Pennants (#S5-028), Classic Squares LG (#S4-126)
- Sizzix Big Shot die-cutting machine
- Paper punches: Martha Stewart Crafts Photo Corner (#M42-25004); ½-inch circle
- Bone folder
- Scotch®/3M Foam Mounting Tape
- Removable tape
- Scor-Pal ¼-inch-wide double-sided adhesive
- Tape
- Tombow Mono Multi liquid glue

Merry & Bright

Materials

- Cardstock: Bazzill Basics (teal); Arjo Wiggins Curious Metallics (ice gold)
- Bo-Bunny Press Snowfall 6 x 6-inch patterned paper pad
- Stamps: Papertrey Ink (Signature Christmas stamp set); Stamp N Plus Scrap N (circle iris-folding pattern #W-IR024 [see Project Note])
- Ink pads: Clearsnap ColorBox (chestnut roan Fluid Chalk); embossing
- Metallic gold embossing powder
- Harmonie Glamor & Mosaic Tiles ⅜-inch dark amber mosaic tile
- 2 tiny blue adhesive rhinestones
- Stampin' Up! Baja Breeze ½-inch-wide teal seam-binding ribbon
- Spellbinders™ die templates: 2011 Heirloom Ornaments (#S4-334), Labels One (#S4-161), Home Sweet Home (#S5-089)
- Sizzix Big Shot die-cutting machine
- Martha Stewart Crafts Ribbon Bow Medium punch (#M283103)
- Spellbinders™ tan embossing mat
- Embossing heat tool
- Bone folder
- Scotch®/3M Foam Mounting Tape
- Removable tape
- Scor-Pal ¼-inch-wide double-sided adhesive
- Tape

Project Note: *If you do not have an iris-folding pattern stamp, use one of the square patterns in this book (pages 47–48).*

1. Form a 5½ x 4¼-inch card from teal cardstock.

2. Cut a 5½ x 1½-inch strip of word patterned paper; ink edges with chalk ink. Layer and adhere onto a 5½ x 1¾-inch strip of ice gold cardstock; adhere to card as shown.

3. For iris-folding frame, die-cut a 3⅞-inch Labels One from center of a 4-inch square of ice gold cardstock. Die-cut and emboss a 2½ x 2⅜-inch 2011 Heirloom Ornament from center of die-cut label.

4. Nest 3⅞-inch and 3⅜-inch Labels One die templates together and die-cut a frame from word pattern paper. Adhere to ice gold frame; ink edges with chalk ink.

5. Stamp iris-folding circle pattern onto scrap paper using chalk ink. Lay frame facedown on stamped pattern, centering pattern in opening; secure with removable tape.

6. Apply double-sided adhesive around edges of opening; peel protective liner strip from adhesive.

7. Cut three ½ x 6-inch strips each from snowflake and mini dot patterned papers. ***Note:*** *Trim away white flourish on mini dot paper.*

8. Disregarding first visible line of pattern on right side, place a snowflake strip right side down at right side of pattern, aligning edge with pattern line. Adhere one end with tape; trim excess and secure opposite end.

9. In the same manner, position mini dot strip at top. Disregarding first visible line on left side of pattern, adhere a snowflake strip at left; adhere a mini dot strip at bottom. Continue working around pattern until six strips have been placed in each section.

10. Adhere a 2½" x 2½" Square of ice gold cardstock to back of center opening using double-sided adhesive.

11. Carefully remove pattern from frame; turn frame panel faceup.

12. Adhere mosaic tile on an angle to center; adhere rhinestone to tile. Punch a bow from word patterned paper; adhere to top of ornament; adhere rhinestone to bow.

13. Wrap ribbon around card front, positioning knot toward left side as shown; trim ends. Stamp sentiment onto ice gold cardstock using embossing ink; sprinkle embossing powder over sentiment and heat-emboss. Die-cut a 1⅜ x ⅞-inch tag around sentiment; adhere to card as shown, tucking end under ribbon knot.

14. Adhere iris-folded panel to card using foam mounting tape. ●

No-Sew Beautiful

Project Note: Directions are given to make an easel card, which will stand on its own. If you prefer, form a standard 5½-inch square card from an 11 x 5½-inch piece of sunflower cardstock; adhere a 5½-inch square of coral cardstock to front, then continue with step 2 of instructions. Work through step 11.

1. Referring to Fig. 1 (page 46), form easel base for card from a 5½ x 11-inch piece of sunflower cardstock by scoring at 2¾ inches and 5½ inches from top. Fold in half at 5½-inch score, then fold back card front at 2¾-inch score (Fig. 2). Adhere a 5½-inch square of coral cardstock to *2¾-inch flap only* so that all edges are even when card is closed.

2. For frame, die-cut a 3½-inch Classic Square LG from center of a 5¼-inch square of sunflower cardstock.

3. Lay frame facedown on 4" x 4" Square Pattern, centering pattern in opening; secure with removable tape.

4. Apply double-sided adhesive around edges of opening; peel protective liner strip from adhesive.

Materials

- 4" x 4" Square Pattern (page 47)
- Bazzill Basics cardstock: coral, sunflower
- Adhesive label paper
- Fabrics: Northcott Studios (Mum's the Word Metallic Sunkissed #NC2684M-26 [raspberry], #NC2685M-53 [gold], #NC2683M-58 [stripe]); Andover Fabrics (Dimples #ANDO1867-G30 [green])
- Mary Ellen's Best Press clear starch alternative
- Adhesive green pearl cabochon
- WonderFil Spotlite light gold metallic thread
- May Arts light green ⅜-inch-wide sheer iridescent pinstripe ribbon
- Spellbinders™ die templates: Classic Scalloped Circles LG (#S4-124), Classic Squares LG (#S4-126)
- Sizzix Big Shot die-cutting machine
- Martha Stewart Crafts Cherish Punch Around the Page border punch set (#40-60044)
- Rotary cutter and mat
- Household iron
- Bone folder
- Scotch®/3M Foam Mounting Tape
- Removable tape
- Scor-Pal ¼-inch-wide double-sided adhesive
- Tape

5. Cut six 5 x 1-inch strips from each fabric; spray with starch, fold in half lengthwise, and press with iron.

6. Referring to Numbering Guide diagram (page 46), place a striped fabric strip at top right, aligning fold with pattern line. Adhere one end with tape; trim excess and secure opposite end. ***Note:*** *To further secure fabric strips, also adhere ends using double-sided adhesive, peeling the protective liner strip when the next strip is attached.*

7. In the same manner, position a green strip at top left; adhere. Adhere a gold strip at bottom left and a raspberry strip at bottom right. Continue working around pattern until six strips have been placed in each section.

8. Die-cut a 2⅝-inch Classic Scalloped Circles LG from coral cardstock. Leaving gold metallic thread on spool, secure thread end on back with tape. Referring to Thread-Wrapping Diagram (page 46) and working from spool, wrap thread around Scallop Circle in "valleys" between individual scallops: Bring thread to front at 1; count nine valleys and take thread to back at 2; bring thread to front at 3 (just to right of 1); count nine valleys and take thread to back at 4, and so on. Continue in this manner until circle is completely wrapped; secure thread end on back with tape.

9. Adhere scalloped circle to back of center opening using double-sided adhesive. Adhere a 5⅛-inch square of label paper over thread-wrapped circle and folded fabric. Carefully remove pattern from frame and turn frame panel faceup. Adhere green pearl to iris center.

10. Wrap ribbon around top of frame as shown; knot. Secure ribbon on back of frame with tape.

11. Center and adhere iris-folded panel to card using foam mounting tape.

12. Border-punch a 5½ x 1-inch strip of sunflower cardstock. Wrap ribbon around width of strip; knot ends near right edge. Adhere to a 5½ x 1½-inch piece of coral cardstock; adhere assembled strips inside card ⅛ inch from bottom edge. ***Note:*** *This strip forms a "stop plate" to hold the easel card open.* ●

Drawings continued on page 46

Tea for Two

Materials

- Triangle Pattern (page 47)
- Bo-Bunny Press patterned papers: Ambrosia, Ambrosia Dot, Ambrosia Flowers, Turquoise Dot double-sided
- Gartner Studios ivory flower table confetti
- Bic Mark-it pens: orange, purple, aqua
- Kaisercraft tiny clear adhesive rhinestones
- Spellbinders™ Nested Tea Cups die templates (#S4-350)
- Sizzix Big Shot die-cutting machine
- Bone folder
- Fiskars mini pinking edgers
- Scotch®/3M Foam Mounting Tape
- Removable tape
- Scor-Pal ¼-inch-wide double-sided adhesive
- Tape
- Glue stick

1. Form a 5½-inch square card from Turquoise Dot paper; set aside.

2. For frame, cut a 5-inch square from Ambrosia paper; die-cut a 3 x 2⅝-inch Nested Tea Cup from center. Die-cut a 1⅛ x 2-inch Handle from Turquoise Dot paper; adhere next to tea cup opening.

3. Position Triangle Pattern on work surface point down. Referring to Aperture Placement Guide, place frame facedown on pattern; secure with removable tape.

4. Apply double-sided adhesive around edges of opening; peel protective liner strip from adhesive.

5. Cut two ½ x 12-inch strips each from Turquoise Dot, Ambrosia Dot and Ambrosia Flowers paper.

6. Place an Ambrosia Dot strip right side down at bottom right, aligning edge with pattern line. Adhere one end with tape; trim excess and secure opposite end.

7. In the same manner, position a Turquoise Dot strip solid side down across top; adhere. Adhere an Ambrosia Flowers strip at bottom left. Continue working around pattern until five strips have been placed in each section.

8. Cut a 2-inch square from Turquoise Dot paper; adhere dotted side down to back of center opening using double-sided adhesive.

9. Carefully remove pattern from frame, and turn frame panel faceup.

10. Using markers, color confetti flowers aqua, orange and purple. Notch ends of petals using mini pinking edgers. Adhere flowers to iris-folded panel as shown.

11. Color one rhinestone each orange and purple; color five rhinestones aqua. Adhere orange, aqua and purple rhinestones to flowers; adhere remaining aqua rhinestones to iris center and in corners of iris-folded panel.

12. Adhere iris-folded panel to card front using foam mounting tape. ●

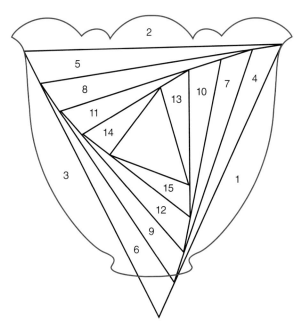

Tea for Two
Aperture Placement Guide

Love in Bloom

Materials

- Octagon Pattern (page 47)
- Cardstock: The Japanese Paper Place (olive, linen); Bazzill Basics (coral); Neenah (flash natural)
- The Japanese Paper Place Chiyogami patterned paper: green-and-white mini pin dot (#802C), pink/yellow/green floral (#602C)
- Gartner Studios pearl brad
- Metallic gold wired mesh ribbon
- Spellbinders™ Large Octagons die templates (#S4-185)
- Sizzix Big Shot die-cutting machine
- Bone folder
- Paper-piercing tool and mat
- Scotch®/3M Foam Mounting Tape
- Removable tape
- Scor-Pal ¼-inch-wide double-sided adhesive
- Tape

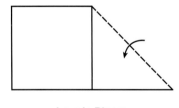

Love in Bloom
Fig. 1

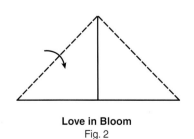

Love in Bloom
Fig. 2

1. Form a 5½-inch-square card from natural cardstock. Adhere a 5⅜-inch square of olive cardstock to card front; set aside.

2. For frame, cut a 4¾-inch square of linen cardstock; die-cut a 2¾-inch Large Octagons from center.

3. Cut four 1 x 2-inch pieces of floral Chiyogami paper; lay facedown. Referring to Fig. 1 and Fig. 2, fold top corners down, aligning edges along bottom and center to form triangles. Slide triangles over corners of iris-folding frame and adhere.

4. Die-cut octagonal border from olive cardstock using 3¾- and 3¼-inch Large Octagons dies nested together. Adhere to frame as shown.

5. Position Octagon Pattern on work surface; place frame facedown on pattern, centering pattern in opening. Secure with removable tape.

6. Apply double-sided adhesive around edges of opening; peel protective liner strip from adhesive.

7. Cut five 1 x 8½-inch strips from pin-dot and floral Chiyogami papers; fold each strip in half lengthwise.

8. Place a floral strip at right side, aligning folded edge with pattern line. Adhere one end with tape; trim excess and secure opposite end.

9. In the same manner, position a pin-dot strip across top; adhere. Adhere a floral strip at left and a pin-dot strip across bottom. Continue working around pattern until five strips have been placed in each section of pattern.

10. Cut a 2½" x 2½" Square of coral cardstock; cut a matching piece of wired mesh ribbon and adhere to right side of cardstock along edges. Lay square, ribbon side down, over center opening and adhere using double-sided adhesive.

11. Carefully remove pattern from frame, and turn frame panel faceup.

12. Pierce hole through iris center; insert pearl brad.

13. Adhere iris-folded panel to card front using foam mounting tape. ●

Potted Wishes

1. Form a 4¼ x 5½-inch card from lagoon cardstock. Adhere a 4 x 5¼-inch piece of white striped paper to card front; set aside.

2. For frame, cut a 3¾ x 5-inch piece of lagoon cardstock. Die-cut a 2⅛ x 1⅞-inch Nested Tea Cup from panel as shown; reserve tea cup die cut.

3. Position Triangle Pattern on work surface point down; referring to Aperture Placement Guide, place frame facedown on pattern; secure with removable tape.

4. Apply double-sided adhesive around edges of opening; peel protective liner strip from adhesive.

5. Cut four ½ x 4½-inch strips each from white, pink and blue Shimmer Sheetz; emboss strips using embossing folder.

6. Place a pink strip right side down at right, aligning edge with pattern line. Adhere one end with tape; trim excess and secure opposite end.

7. In the same manner, position a white strip across top; adhere. Adhere a blue strip at bottom left. Continue working around pattern until four strips have been placed in each section of pattern.

8. Adhere reserved tea cup die cut from step 2 to back of center opening using double-sided adhesive. Adhere a 3⅜-inch square of label paper over entire iris-folded design.

9. Carefully remove pattern from frame; turn frame faceup and adhere to card front using foam mounting tape.

Materials

- Triangle Pattern (page 47)
- Cardstock: Stardream pearlescent (lagoon); kraft, white
- WorldWin Pearlescent white-on-white stripe patterned paper
- Elizabeth Craft Shimmer Sheetz™: white iris, pink iris, blue iris
- Adhesive label paper
- Kaisercraft tiny white adhesive pearls
- ⅛-inch-wide white satin ribbon
- Die templates: Spellbinders™ (Nested Tea Cups #S4-350, Flower Pots #S5-060); Provo Craft Cuttlebug A2 Combo (Friends Forever #37-1166)
- Stampin' Up! Lattice Textured Impressions embossing folder (#119976)
- Sizzix Big Shot die-cutting machine
- Martha Stewart Crafts Frond medium punch (#M283047)
- Bone folder
- Scotch®/3M Foam Mounting Tape
- Xyron sticker maker
- Removable tape
- Scor-Pal ¼-inch-wide double-sided adhesive
- Tape

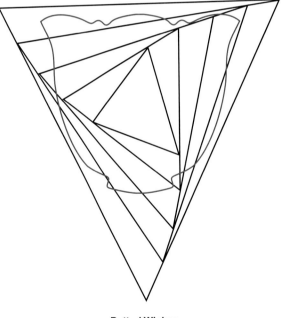

Potted Wishes
Aperture Placement Guide

10. Punch two fronds from unembossed blue Shimmer Sheetz; apply adhesive using Xyron machine. Adhere fronds to card front as shown.

11. Die-cut a 2⅝ x 1⅝-inch plant pot from kraft cardstock; score pot at indentations; fold down along scored line to form pot rim. Secure rim with foam mounting tape. Tie ribbon around pot rim; adhere pot to card as shown.

12. Die-cut sentiment from white cardstock; apply adhesive with Xyron machine and adhere to card front as shown. Adhere pearl to iris center and another to dot the "i" in sentiment. ●

Home Is the Heart

Materials

- 2" x 2" Square Pattern (page 48)
- Michaels Recollections red cardstock
- Patterned papers: Bazzill Basics Antique Book Paper (Antique Dictionary Page, Antique Sheet Music, Antique Letter, Antique Ledger Paper); Little Yellow Bicycle (Swoon Black Tie Stripe/Special Day)
- Stardream anthracite text-weight paper
- Quietfire Design Home Is the Heart stamp
- Clearsnap ColorBox flannel gray Ancient Page dye ink
- ½-inch red heart rhinestone
- Spellbinders™ die templates: Home Sweet Home (#S5-089), Classic Squares LG (#S4-126)
- Sizzix Big Shot die-cutting machine
- Punches: Martha Stewart Crafts (Fence Edger #MS875145); Fiskars (¼-inch heart #23607097)
- Bone folder
- Scotch®/3M Foam Mounting Tape
- Scor-Pal ¼-inch-wide double-sided adhesive
- Removable tape
- Tape

1. Form a 5½ x 4¼-inch card from red cardstock. Center and adhere a 5¼ x 4-inch piece of anthracite paper to card front; set card aside.

2. For frame, cut a 5 x 3¾-inch piece of red cardstock; referring to photo, die-cut a 2-inch Classic Squares LG in lower left corner.

3. Position 2" x 2" Square Pattern on work surface. Place frame facedown on pattern, centering pattern in opening; secure with removable tape.

4. Apply double-sided adhesive around edges of opening; peel protective liner strip from adhesive.

5. Cut five 1 x 4-inch strips each from Antique Dictionary Page, Antique Sheet Music, Antique Letter and Antique Ledger papers; fold in half lengthwise.

6. Place an Antique Dictionary strip at lower right, aligning folded edge with pattern line. Adhere one end with tape; trim excess and secure opposite end.

7. In the same manner, position an Antique Ledger Page strip across upper right; adhere. Adhere an Antique Sheet Music strip at upper left and an Antique Letter strip at lower left. Continue working around pattern until all areas are filled except center square.

8. Adhere a 2-inch square of anthracite paper to back of center opening. Carefully remove pattern from frame; turn frame panel faceup and adhere heart rhinestone to iris center.

9. Die-cut Home Sweet Home roof and punch a 5-inch picket fence border from Swoon Black Tie Stripe paper; trim picket fence to ⅝-inch wide. Adhere to iris-folded panel as shown.

10. Stamp sentiment onto a 1⅜ x 2½-inch piece of Antique Ledger paper; adhere to anthracite paper and trim, leaving a ⅛-inch border. Adhere to card as shown using double-sided adhesive. Punch a heart from red cardstock; adhere to sentiment over "a" in "heart."

11. Adhere iris-folded panel to card using foam mounting tape. ●

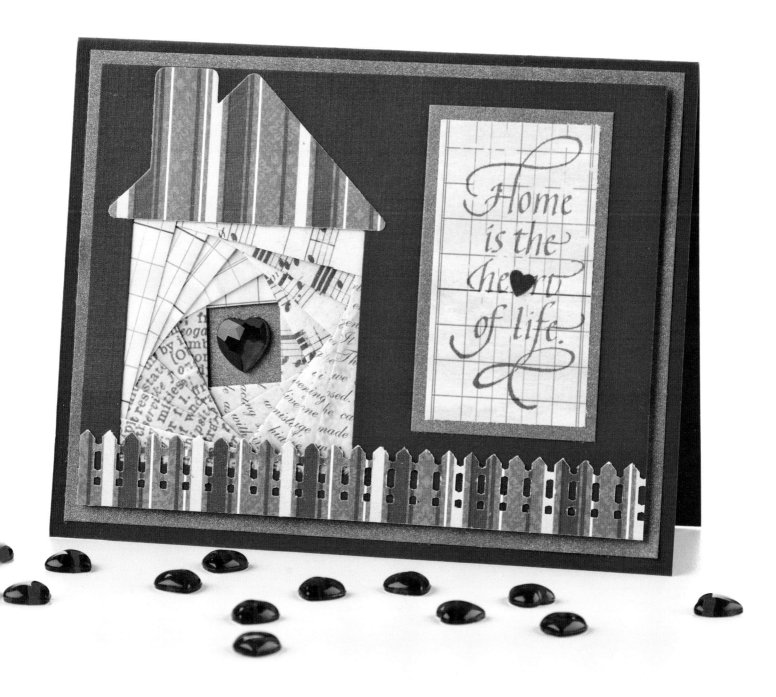

Lucky Li'l Ladybug

Materials

- 4" x 4" Square Pattern (page 47)
- Bazzill Basics Bling light blue cardstock
- The Japanese Paper Place Chiyogami patterned paper
- Paplin ½-inch pearl purple quilling strips
- Tiny adhesive rhinestones: lavender and red flowers, black round
- Wonderfil holographic metallic thread
- Spellbinders™ die templates: Standard Circles LG (#S4-114), Labels Twenty-Two (#S4-346)
- Sizzix Big Shot die-cutting machine
- Bone folder
- Tweezers
- Scotch®/3M Foam Mounting Tape
- Removable tape
- Scor-Pal ¼-inch-wide double-sided adhesive
- Tape

1. Form a 5½-inch-square card from light blue cardstock. Adhere 5-inch square of Chiyogami paper to card front; set aside.

2. For frame, die-cut a 3⅞ x 4⅛-inch Labels Twenty-Two from light blue cardstock; die-cut a 2¾-inch Standard Circles LG from center.

3. Position 4" x 4" Square Pattern on work surface; place frame facedown on pattern, centering pattern in opening. Secure with removable tape.

4. Apply double-sided adhesive around edges of opening; peel protective liner strip from adhesive.

5. Cut six 1 x 8½-inch strips from patterned paper; fold in half lengthwise. Approximately two quilling strips will be needed.

6. Place quilling strip at bottom right, aligning edge with pattern line. Adhere one end with tape; trim excess and secure opposite end.

7. In the same manner, position a patterned paper strip at top right; adhere. Adhere a quilling strip at top left, and a patterned paper strip at bottom left. Continue working around pattern until all areas are filled except center square. (There will be six strips in each quadrant.)

8. Carefully remove frame from pattern and turn frame panel faceup. Cut a 2-inch square of patterned paper with ladybug in center; adhere facedown to back of center opening.

9. Leaving thread on spool, secure thread end on back of iris-folded panel with tape. Referring to photo throughout, wrap thread around sides of frame; clip and secure thread end on back.

10. Adhere clusters of one red and two purple rhinestone flowers to top and bottom of iris-folded frame; adhere single black rhinestone to center (red) flower in each group. Adhere black rhinestones to black spots on ladybug in center of iris-folded design.

11. Adhere iris-folded panel to card front as shown using foam mounting tape. ●

Your Special Day

Materials

- 2" x 2" Square Pattern (page 48)
- Cardstock: Bazzill Basics (white smooth); Stardream Metallic (anthracite, rose quartz)
- Little Yellow Bicycle Swoon Black Tie Stripe/Special Day patterned paper
- Stardream Metallic text-weight papers: anthracite, rose quartz
- Gina K. Designs stamp sets: Framed Greetings, Botanicals
- Clearsnap flannel gray Ancient Page dye ink pad
- Michaels tiny charcoal adhesive rhinestones
- May Arts ⅜-inch-wide charcoal sheer iridescent pinstripe ribbon
- Spellbinders™ Standard Circles SM die templates (#S4-116)
- Sizzix Big Shot die-cutting machine
- EK Success ⁹⁄₁₆-inch flower punch
- Bone folder
- Scotch®/3M Foam Mounting Tape
- Removable tape
- Scor-Pal ¼-inch-wide double-sided adhesive
- Tape
- Tombow Mono Multi liquid glue

1. Form a 5½ x 4¼-inch card from patterned paper with polka-dot side facing out.

2. Referring to photo throughout, adhere a 5½ x 3-inch piece of rose quartz cardstock to card front. Tie ribbon around card front, positioning knot toward right-hand edge; set card aside.

3. For frame, stamp striped image onto a 2⅞ x 3-inch piece of white cardstock. Die-cut a 1⅝-inch Standard Circles SM from center of stamped image.

4. Position 2" x 2" Square Pattern on work surface; place frame facedown on pattern, centering pattern in opening. Secure with removable tape.

5. Apply double-sided adhesive around edges of opening; peel protective liner strip from adhesive.

6. Cut eight ½ x 6-inch strips from white cardstock; stamp four with floral image and four with script image from stamp sets. Cut four ½ x 3-inch strips each from anthracite and rose quartz metallic cardstocks.

7. Place rose quartz strip at bottom right, aligning edge with pattern line. Adhere one end with tape; trim excess and secure opposite end.

8. In the same manner, position a stamped floral strip at top right, right side down; adhere. Adhere an anthracite strip at top left and a stamped script strip at bottom left. Continue working around pattern until all areas are filled except center square.

9. Adhere a 1½-inch square of patterned paper over opening in iris center with polka-dot side facedown. Carefully remove frame from pattern and turn frame panel faceup.

10. Punch six flowers from rose quartz cardstock; adhere a rhinestone to center of each flower using liquid glue; adhere one flower to center of iris; cluster remaining flowers along right edge of opening.

11. Adhere a 3⅜-inch square of rose quartz paper to a 3⅝-inch square of anthracite paper. Cut out "Special Day" sentiment from patterned paper and adhere to back of layered paper squares along right-hand edge; adhere to card front as shown.

12. Adhere iris-folded panel to layered paper squares on card front using foam mounting tape. ●

Thanks So Much

Materials

- 2" x 2" Square Variation Pattern (page 48)
- Bazzill Basics cardstock: ivory, green, brown
- Graphic 45 Little Darlings Cherished patterned paper
- Dictionary pages
- Gina K. Designs Framed Greetings stamp set
- Clearsnap ColorBox warm red Fluid Chalk ink pad
- Making Memories mini heart brad
- Spellbinders™ die templates: Nested Apples (#S4-267), Nested Pennants (#S5-028)
- Crafts-Too Hearts embossing folder (#CTFD3018)
- Sizzix Big Shot die-cutting machine
- Bone folder
- Paper-piercing tool and mat
- Scotch®/3M Foam Mounting Tape
- Removable tape
- Scor-Pal ¼-inch-wide double-sided adhesive

1. Form a 5½ x 4¼-inch card from green cardstock.

2. Cut a 3 x 3¾-inch piece of ivory cardstock; emboss with hearts.

3. Adhere embossed rectangle to card front as shown using double-sided adhesive.

4. Cut a 3 x 4¼-inch piece of patterned paper; adhere to card as shown.

5. Stamp sentiment onto smooth side of ivory cardstock. Die-cut a Nested Pennant Ribbon shape around sentiment leaving a ⅞-inch margin along right side. Adhere sentiment to card front as shown using double-sided adhesive. Set card aside.

6. Cut three ½ x 12-inch strips from patterned paper; cut ten 1-inch strips from dictionary page that are at least 3 inches long. Fold dictionary-print strips in half lengthwise.

7. For frame, cut a 2¾-inch square of green cardstock. Die-cut a 1¾-inch-wide Nested Apple from center.

8. Place apple frame facedown on 2" x 2" Square Variation Pattern with pattern centered in opening; secure with removable tape.

9. Apply double-sided adhesive around edges of opening; peel protective liner strip from tape.

10. Cut a ⅜ x ¾-inch piece from brown cardstock; apply across frame over apple stem.

11. Place polka-dot strip right side down at bottom right, aligning edge with pattern line. Adhere one end with tape; trim excess and secure opposite end.

12. In the same manner, position a dictionary-print strip right side down at top right; adhere. Adhere polka-dot strip at top left and dictionary-print strip at bottom left. Continue working around pattern until all areas are filled except for center square.

13. Cut a 2-inch square from green cardstock; adhere to back of center opening using double-sided adhesive.

14. Carefully remove pattern from frame and turn frame faceup.

15. Pierce hole through iris center; insert brad.

16. Adhere iris-folded panel to card front as shown with foam mounting tape. ●

So Happy

Materials

- 2½" x 2½" Square Pattern (page 47)
- Bazzill Basics cardstock: brown, ivory
- My Mind's Eye Stella & Rose Hazel Fancy Lots of Dots patterned paper
- Stardream lagoon text-weight paper
- Stampin' Up! Petite Pairs stamp set
- Ink: Ranger (vintage photo Distress pad, hazelnut Adirondack alcohol); Imagine Crafts/Tsukineko (8ml walnut ink spritzer); Clearsnap ColorBox Fluid Chalk (chestnut roan)
- Nylon zippers: 1 brown, 1 turquoise
- 8 inches Cheep Trims ⅜-inch-wide Measuring Tape printed twill tape
- ½-inch snap
- Spellbinders™ die templates: Standard Circles LG (#S4-114), Standard Circles SM (#S4-116)
- Sizzix Big Shot die-cutting machine
- Bone folder
- Sponge
- Embossing heat tool (optional)
- Scotch®/3M Foam Mounting Tape
- Adhesive dot
- Removable tape
- Scor-Pal ¼-inch-wide double-sided adhesive
- Tape

1. Form a 4¼ x 5½-inch card from brown cardstock; set aside.

2. For frame, die-cut a 2⅜-inch Standard Circles LG from center of a 3¾ x 5-inch piece of Lots of Dots paper. Apply distress ink to outer edges of cardstock using sponge.

3. Lay frame facedown on 2½" x 2½" Square Pattern, centering pattern in window. Secure with removable tape.

4. Apply double-sided adhesive around edges of opening; peel protective liner strip from adhesive.

5. Trim nylon zipper teeth from zippers, retaining fabric edging. Working from length of zipper fabric, position brown strip in lower right, aligning finished edge of fabric with line on pattern. Adhere one end with tape; trim excess and adhere opposite end.

6. In the same manner, position turquoise zipper in upper right quadrant. ***Note:*** *In addition to tape, secure zipper layers using double-sided adhesive, removing liner before next strip is applied. Adhere a brown strip in upper left area and a turquoise strip in lower left.*

7. Continue working around pattern until four strips of zipper fabric have been placed in each section.

8. Cut a 2¼-inch square from Lots of Dots paper; adhere facedown over iris opening. Carefully remove pattern from frame and turn faceup.

9. Die-cut a ⅝-inch Standard Circles SM from lagoon paper; adhere to Lots of Dots paper in iris center. Using alcohol ink, color surface of snap half with peg facing up; adhere to lagoon paper circle using adhesive dot.

10. Spritz twill tape with walnut ink, and lay flat to dry. ***Notes:*** *Place tape in a box lid to avoid overspraying surrounding area. Speed drying with a heat tool.* Adhere twill tape along left edge of iris-folded panel, adhering ends on back. Adhere panel to card as shown using foam mounting tape.

11. Stamp sentiment onto smooth side of ivory cardstock using chalk ink; die-cut a 1⅛-inch Standard Circles SM around sentiment and ink edges using distress ink and sponge.

12. Die-cut a 1⅛-inch Standard Circles SM from lagoon paper; adhere stamped circle to lagoon circle as shown, offsetting circles slightly. Adhere to card using double-sided adhesive and foam mounting tape. ●

Miss You

Materials

- 2½" x 2½" Square Pattern (page 47)
- Cardstock: Michaels Recollections (red, bronze metallic); Neenah (flash natural)
- The Japanese Paper Place floral print (#727C) Chiyogami patterned paper
- Gina K. Designs Botanicals stamp set
- Clearsnap ColorBox chestnut roan Fluid Chalk ink pad
- May Arts ½-inch-wide shimmer ivory woven ribbon
- ¾-inch ivory satin daisy
- Michaels Recollections antique copper brads: small, tiny
- Spellbinders™ die templates: Standard Circles SM (#S4-116), Persian Motifs (#S5-079)
- Sizzix Big Shot die-cutting machine
- Bone folder
- Paper-piercing tool
- Embossing heat tool and mat
- Scotch®/3M Foam Mounting Tape
- Removable tape
- Scor-Pal ¼-inch-wide double-sided adhesive
- Tape

1. Form a 4¼ x 5½-inch card from bronze metallic cardstock; set aside.

2. For frame, die-cut a 4-inch Persian Motif from natural cardstock. Die-cut a 2⅛-inch Standard Circles SM from center of motif; reserve circle. Adhere motif to a 4 x 5¼-inch piece of red cardstock as shown; secure additionally with removable tape. Die-cut a 2⅛-inch circle from red cardstock in center of motif and reserve.

3. Pierce Persian Motif and cardstock at base of each "petal"; attach tiny brads.

4. Lay frame facedown on 2½" x 2½" Square Pattern, centering pattern in opening; secure with removable tape.

5. Apply double-sided adhesive around edges of opening; peel protective liner strip from adhesive.

6. Cut two or three ½ x 12-inch strips from bronze metallic cardstock. Cut four 1 x 8-inch strips from Chiyogami paper; fold in half lengthwise and burnish creases with bone folder.

7. Position Chiyogami strip right side down at bottom right, aligning folded edge with line on pattern. Adhere one end with tape; trim excess and adhere opposite end.

8. In the same manner, position a bronze strip at top right, aligning edge with line on pattern. Adhere a Chiyogami strip at top left and a bronze strip at bottom left.

9. Continue working around pattern until all areas are filled except center square; four strips will be applied in each section.

10. Adhere reserved red die-cut circle from step 2 facedown over opening in iris. Carefully remove pattern from frame and turn faceup. Remove removable tape.

11. Adhere satin flower to square in iris center; pierce flower and cardstock and attach small brad.

12. Tie ribbon around bottom of iris-folded panel as shown; position knot toward left side and trim ribbon ends. Adhere iris-folded panel to card using double-sided adhesive.

13. Stamp sentiment onto reserved natural cardstock circle from step 2; set and dry ink with heat tool. Die-cut a 1⅛-inch circle around sentiment; adhere to ribbon in right corner using foam mounting tape. ●

Love

1. Form a 5½-inch-square card from black cardstock. Center and adhere a 5¼ x 5½-inch piece of Tiki Voyager paper to card front; set card aside.

2. Emboss a 4¼ x 5½-inch piece of natural cardstock using embossing folder. For frame, use a craft knife and metal-edge ruler to cut rectangular window from center of cardstock piece, following embossed lines; set aside cutout rectangle.

3. Lay embossed frame facedown on 2½" x 2½" Square Pattern, centering pattern in window as shown on Aperture Placement & Numbering Guide; secure with removable tape.

Materials

- 2½" x 2½" Square Pattern (page 47)
- Cardstock: The Paper Company™/ TPC Studio™ (black linen); Neenah (flash natural)
- Patterned papers: Graphic 45 (Tropical Travelogue Tiki Voyager); Michaels Recollections (Script Cream)
- Technique Tuesday Perspectives by Ali Edwards stamp set
- Clearsnap ColorBox chestnut roan Fluid Chalk ink pad
- Instant coffee crystals
- 6mm adhesive topaz rhinestone
- ½-inch-wide scalloped crochet edging
- Provo Craft Cuttlebug Flourished Frame embossing folder (#37-1912)
- Sizzix Big Shot die-cutting machine
- Oval cutter
- Bone folder
- Craft knife
- Metal-edge ruler
- Embossing heat tool (optional)
- Scotch®/3M Foam Mounting Tape
- Removable tape
- Scor-Pal ¼-inch-wide double-sided adhesive
- Tape

4. Apply double-sided adhesive around edges of opening; peel protective liner strip from adhesive.

5. Cut four ½ x 12-inch strips from Tiki Voyager paper; cut five 1 x 8-inch strips from Script Cream paper. Fold 1-inch strips in half lengthwise.

6. ***Note:*** *Disregard horizontal lines at very top and bottom of Aperture Placement & Numbering Guide, and begin placing strips in those sections against next line.* Referring to Aperture Placement & Numbering Guide throughout, position a Tiki Voyager strip facedown in lower right at position 1, aligning edge with line on pattern. Adhere one end with tape; trim excess and adhere opposite end.

7. Position a Script Cream strip in upper right at position 2, aligning folded edge with line on pattern. In the same manner, adhere a Tiki Voyager strip in upper left at position 3 and a Script Cream strip in lower left at position 4.

8. Continue working pattern in numerical order until all areas are filled except center square. ***Note:*** *Follow order on Numbering Guide carefully. There will be five Tiki Voyager strips in the lower right (1, 5, 9, 13, 15) and upper left (3, 7, 11, 14, 17) sections, and four Cream Script strips in the upper right (2, 6, 10, 16) and lower left (4, 8, 12, 18) sections.*

9. Adhere reserved embossed rectangle from step 2 to back of center opening using double-sided adhesive.

10. Carefully remove pattern from frame and turn frame faceup. Adhere rhinestone to embossed center square.

11. "Age" crochet trim by soaking it in a mixture of coffee crystals and hot water until desired color is achieved. Squeeze out excess moisture and lay trim flat on waxed paper to dry. ***Note:*** *Speed up drying time with a heat tool.*

12. Adhere trim along edge of iris-folded panel as shown; adhere panel to card using foam mounting tape.

13. Stamp sentiment onto natural cardstock. Cut a 2 x ⅞-inch oval around sentiment; adhere to a 2¼ x ⅞-inch oval cut from Tiki Voyager paper. Adhere ovals to card as shown using foam mounting tape. ●

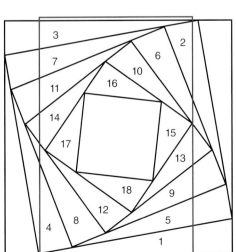

Love
Aperture Placement & Numbering Guide

Gratitude

Materials

- 2" x 2" Square Variation Pattern (page 48)
- Bazzill Basics cardstock: aqua, brown, ivory
- My Mind's Eye Stella & Rose Hazel Fancy Lots of Dots patterned paper
- Stardream ivory text-weight paper
- Stamps: Penny Black Inc. (Gratitude); Hero Arts Clings (Four Flowers set)
- Ink pads: Ranger Distress (vintage photo); Clearsnap ColorBox Fluid Chalk (chestnut roan)
- Teal permanent marker
- 5mm clear adhesive rhinestone
- Die templates: Spellbinders™ (Standard Circles LG #S4-114, Lacey Circles #S4-293); Memory Box/Poppystamps (Tilda Swirl #804)
- Sizzix Big Shot die-cutting machine
- Bone folder
- Sponge
- Removable tape
- Scor-Pal ¼-inch-wide double-sided adhesive
- Tape

1. Form a 4¼ x 5½-inch card from Lots of Dots paper. Ink edges with distress ink using sponge; let dry.

2. Adhere a 1 x 5½-inch strip of brown cardstock near fold as shown.

3. Mask bottom of Gratitude stamp with removable tape. Ink stamp with chalk ink; remove tape and stamp sentiment onto smooth side of ivory cardstock. Cut a rectangle around sentiment and adhere to card as shown. Set card aside.

4. For frame, stamp a 2½-inch flower onto a 3½-inch square of aqua cardstock using chalk ink. Die-cut a 1⅜-inch Standard Circles LG from flower center. *Note: You can die-cut the larger circle around the frame at this point or, as the designer has done, after the iris-folded design has been completed (step 11). If your die-cutting machine will not accommodate the extra layers of iris-folded strips, complete step 11 now, then resume with step 5.*

5. Lay frame facedown on 2" x 2" Square Variation Pattern, centering pattern in opening; secure with removable tape.

6. Apply double-sided adhesive around edges of opening; peel protective liner strip from adhesive.

7. Cut three 12 x ½-inch strips from Lots of Dots cardstock; cut three 11 x ½-inch strips from ivory paper.

8. Position a Lots of Dots strip right side down at bottom right, aligning edge with line on pattern. Adhere one end with tape; trim excess and adhere opposite end.

9. In the same manner, position an ivory strip at top right and adhere. Adhere a Lots of Dots strip at top left and an ivory strip at bottom left.

10. Continue working around pattern until all areas are filled except center square. Carefully remove pattern from frame and turn faceup. Remove tape.

11. Die-cut a 2¾-inch Standard Circles LG around iris-folded panel.

12. Die-cut a 1⅞-inch Lacey Circles from brown cardstock; die-cut a 1⅜-inch Standard Circles LG from center of Lacey Circle and retain. Adhere Lacey Circle over stamped flower on iris-folded frame. Adhere reserved brown circle to back of center opening of iris-folded design using double-sided adhesive. Color rhinestone with marker; adhere to center of iris-folded design.

13. Die-cut two Tilda Swirls from ivory cardstock; layer together, alternating positions of petals, and adhere. Layer iris-folded panel onto swirls; adhere to card front as shown. ●

Happy for You

Materials

- 2" x 2" Square Pattern (page 48)
- Arjo Wiggins Curious Metallics ice gold cardstock
- Graphic 45 Little Darlings patterned papers: Little Treasures, Heaven Sent
- Gina K. Designs Botanicals stamp set
- Clearsnap ColorBox rose coral Fluid Chalk ink pad
- Copic® marker: R01
- ⅛-inch ivory adhesive pearls
- ⅜-inch-wide white satin ribbon
- Spellbinders™ Fair Isle Pendants die templates (#S4-270)
- Sizzix Big Shot die-cutting machine
- Bone folder
- Embossing heat tool
- Stylus
- EK Success flower punch
- Scotch®/3M Foam Mounting Tape
- Scor-Pal ¼-inch-wide double-sided adhesive
- Removable tape
- Tape

1. Form a 4¼ x 5½-inch card from Heaven Sent patterned paper. Adhere a 3¾ x 5½-inch piece of ice gold cardstock to card as shown; set card aside.

2. Cut a 4-inch square of ice gold cardstock; die-cut using 3½-inch-square Pendant and 1⅝-inch-square center Fair Isle Pendants die templates at the same time, forming a pendant-shape frame. Ink inner edge of frame using marker.

3. Adhere die-cut frame to peach side of a 3½ x 5½-inch piece of Little Treasures patterned paper as shown. Die-cut peach paper in center of frame using 1⅝-inch-square center Fair Isle Pendants die template.

4. Place frame facedown on 2" x 2" Square Pattern with pattern centered in opening; secure with removable tape.

5. Apply double-sided adhesive around edges of opening; peel protective liner strip from tape.

6. Color 20 inches of ribbon using marker, applying two coats; let dry.

7. Working from spool, position white ribbon at bottom right of pattern, aligning ribbon edge with pattern line. Adhere one end with tape; trim excess and secure opposite end.

8. In the same manner, working with 20-inch length, position peach ribbon at top right; adhere. Adhere white ribbon at top left and peach ribbon at bottom left. Continue working around pattern until three strips have been applied in each section.

9. Carefully remove pattern from frame.

10. Stamp sentiment onto a 2-inch square of cardstock; dry with heat tool. ***Note:*** *Using the heat tool speeds the drying process and sets the ink on the lightly coated cardstock.* Center and adhere sentiment in iris.

11. Die-cut Accent 2 decorative motif from cardstock. Cut a 4-inch length of peach ribbon; thread ends from front to back through center holes in motif. Crisscross ribbon ends on back and thread ribbon ends through holes from back to front, using stylus as needed to push ribbon through openings. Trim ribbon ends at an angle as shown; adhere motif to card front below frame with foam mounting tape.

12. Punch six flowers from Little Treasures patterned paper; adhere to frame as shown. Adhere a pearl to center of each flower. ●

Follow Your Dreams

Materials

- Cardstock: Stardream (amber); Bazzill Basics (ivory)
- Graphic 45 Little Darlings Heaven Sent patterned paper
- Stardream Amber text-weight paper
- Paplin ½-inch-wide pearlescent quilling strips: pearl blue, pearl green
- Quietfire Design Follow Your Dreams stamp
- Embossing ink pad
- Gold embossing powder
- 24-gauge gold wire
- 8 Kaisercraft light green adhesive rhinestones in graduated sizes, 3mm–5mm
- Spellbinders™ die templates: Nested Butterflies Two (#S4-320); Standard Circles LG (#S4-114)
- Provo Craft Cuttlebug Swiss Dots embossing folder (#37-1604)
- Sizzix Big Shot die-cutting machine
- Spellbinders™ tan embossing mat
- Bone folder
- Embossing heat tool
- Wire-twisting tool
- Pliers: needle-nose, round-nose
- Wooden skewer
- Scotch®/3M Foam Mounting Tape
- Scor-Pal ¼-inch-wide double-sided adhesive
- Removable tape
- Tape
- Ranger Glossy Accents

1. Form a 4¼ x 5½-inch card from butterfly side of patterned paper. Center and adhere a 4 x 5¼-inch piece of Amber paper to card; set aside.

2. Cut a 3¾ x 5-inch piece of patterned paper. Referring to photo, create frame by die-cutting a 2¼ x 2-inch Nested Butterflies Two butterfly at an angle, toward top of paper.

3. Place frame facedown on Numbering Guide, which doubles as iris-folding pattern; secure with removable tape.

4. Apply double-sided adhesive around edges of opening; peel protective liner strip from tape.

5. Cut five 4-inch pieces from blue and green quilling strips; emboss dots using embossing folder.

6. Position a green strip embossed side down at base of right-hand butterfly wing (1), aligning strip edge with pattern line at tip of wing. Adhere one end with tape; trim excess and secure opposite end.

7. In the same manner, position another green strip at bottom left wing (2); adhere. Adhere blue strip at next line on right (3) and another blue strip at next line on left (4). Continue in this manner, alternating colors and following numbered order, until wings have been filled. Adhere a green strip across remaining V-shape opening at top.

8. Carefully remove pattern from frame; turn faceup.

9. Referring to photo throughout, adhere rhinestones down center of butterfly from largest (head) to smallest.

10. For tail, fold a 10-inch piece of wire in half; insert skewer at fold and twist. Holding cut ends of wire with pliers, rotate skewer to twist wires together down their length. Remove skewer; clip off loop and wire ends. Using pliers, coil wire at one end (Fig. 1). Adhere tail to card using craft cement.

11. For antennae, fold a ¾-inch piece of wire lightly at center. Form loops at each end using round- or needle-nose pliers (Fig. 2). Adhere antennae to card using craft cement.

12. Stamp sentiment onto amber cardstock; emboss. Die-cut a 2⅜-inch circle around sentiment; adhere to card as shown using foam mounting tape.

13. Die-cut and emboss three 1 x ⅞-inch Nested Butterflies Two butterflies from amber cardstock. Adhere to card as shown using foam mounting tape. ●

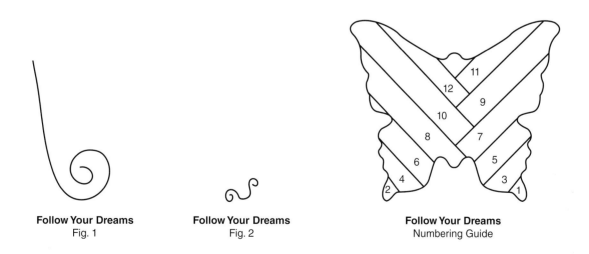

Follow Your Dreams
Fig. 1

Follow Your Dreams
Fig. 2

Follow Your Dreams
Numbering Guide

No-Sew Beautiful

continued from page 19

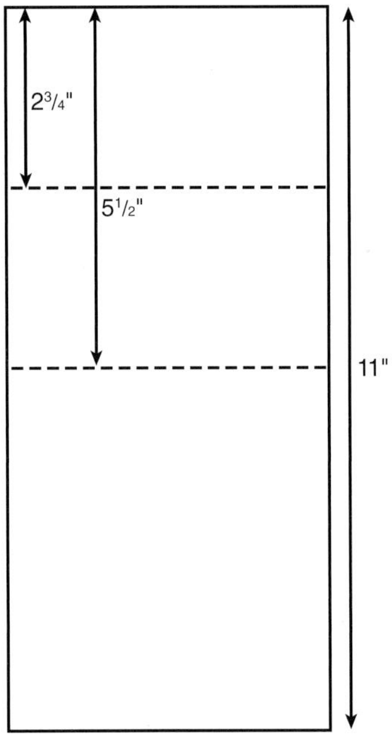

No-Sew Beautiful
Fig. 1

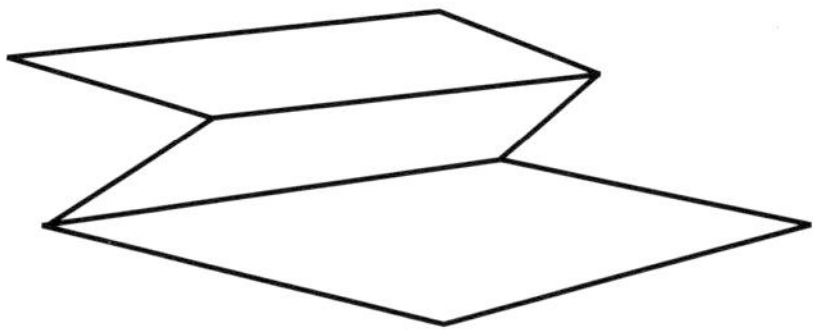

No-Sew Beautiful
Fig. 2

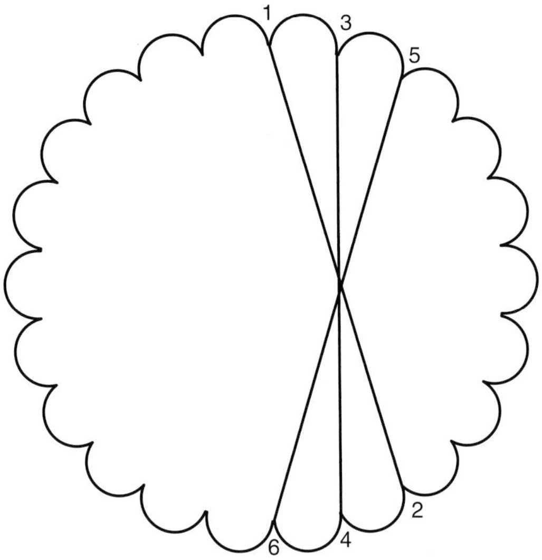

No-Sew Beautiful
Thread-Wrapping Diagram

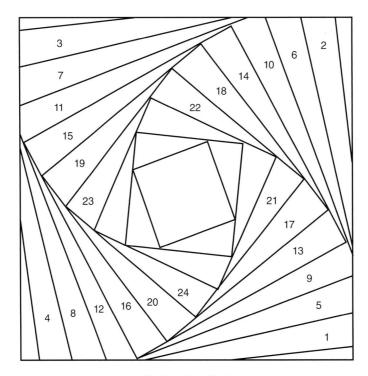

No-Sew Beautiful
Numbering Guide